John Diefenbaker

#13

The outsider who refused to quit

Written by Lanny Boutin

Illustrated by Gabriel Morrissette

Photo Credits
JackFruit Press would like to thank Martin Devenyi for
images appearing on pages 9, 15, 21, 25 , 29, and 35;
the Canadian National Archives for permission to print
the photograph on page 27; and Getty Images for Paula
Bronstein's photograph on page 19 and Per-Anders
Pettersson's photograph of Nelson Mandela appearing
on page 23. We would also like to thank Robert Paul of
the Diefenbaker Canada Centre for sending us the
"Diefenbuck" image that appears on page 38.

© 2006 JackFruit Press Ltd.
Publisher — Jacqueline Brown
Editors — Jacqueline Brown and Patricia Visser
Designer and Art Director — Marcel Lafleur
Researchers — Barbara Baillargeon, Hagit Hadaya, and
Peter Konieczny

JackFruit Press Ltd.
Toronto, Canada
www.jackfruitpress.com

Library and Archives Canada Cataloguing in
Publication

Boutin, Lanny, 1958-   .
John Diefenbaker: The outsider who refused to quit /
Lanny Boutin; illustrator, Gabriel Morrissette.

(Canadian prime ministers: warts and all)
Includes index.
ISBN 0-9736406-4-2

1. Diefenbaker, John G., 1895–1979—Juvenile literature.
2. Canada—Politics and government—1957–1963—
Juvenile literature.
3. Prime ministers—Canada—Biography—Juvenile
literature.
I. Morrissette, Gabriel, 1959- II. Title. III. Series.

FC616.D53B69 2006   j971.064'2'092
C2005-907790-5

Printed and bound in Canada

...So, I'm here to show you around this really cool series of books on great Canadians.

This book tells the story of John Diefenbaker, Canada's 13th prime minister.

He was an outsider who devoted his life to defending the rights of the underdog —other outsiders like him.

Contents

The outsider who made it inside 4

Just a farmer's son 8

John discovers his passion 14

Passing the bar 20

Try, try, and try again 24

In the House at last 28

Finally in charge of the country 34

Chief no more 40

John Diefenbaker: He never stopped fighting 46

Timeline:
The life and times of John Diefenbaker 48

Glossary:
Words and facts you might want to know 52

Index:
Where to find stuff in this book 5 6

Hot topics

The many casualties of war 19
Defending human rights all over the world 23
The Great Depression in the Prairies 27
The Cold War and the Cuban missile crisis 37
The strange and sad story of the Avro Arrow 43

John Diefenbaker: The outsider

GIVE US A BILL OF RIGHTS !!!

NO to NUCLEAR NATIONAL HEAL C.

NO!

GIVE US A REAL BUCK, NOT A DIEFENBUCK!!!

NO NUCLEAR WEAPONS FOR CANADA!

Have you ever felt like the whole world was against you? What if you were the top dog, the head honcho—the prime minister of Canada—and it seemed like every single person in the country wanted you to move to outer space? Wouldn't be much fun, would it? Well, that's exactly the situation Canada's 13th prime minister found himself in, back in 1962.

who made it inside

Have you ever felt like the whole world was against you? What if you were the top dog, the head honcho—the prime minister of Canada—and it seemed like every single person in the country wanted you to move to outer space? Wouldn't be much fun, would it? Well, that's exactly the situation John George Diefenbaker found himself in, back in 1962.

Too bold an ambition?

He was only following his dream—a dream that he'd had since he was eight or nine, when he declared to his mom that someday he would be prime minister. She tried to let him down gently. She felt it was too bold an ambition for a poor Saskatchewan farm boy. But John just would not be put off—he knew one day he would lead Canada.

John grew up to be a fiery Saskatchewan lawyer with piercing, steel-blue eyes. People came from miles around to hear him speak. He fought his way through five elections, finally winning a **seat in Parliament** on his sixth try! It took another 17 years for John to win the prime minister's chair.

Want to know more? The words in bold are explained in the glossary at the back of the book.

Politicians in the 1950s were supposed to be modest and restrained, but that wasn't John's way. John had an intense, penetrating stare and a thunderous voice, and he spoke with great intensity and fire. When he spoke he would draw himself up to his full height—which at six feet two was pretty impressive—and, with one hand on his hip, he'd use the other to thump the table or, most often, to point directly at his target. His jowls shook and that pointing finger jabbed at his victim with every word he bellowed out. Prime Minister **William Lyon Mackenzie King** once complained to John, "You strike me to the heart, every time you speak." Even members of his own party sometimes wished he'd sit down and shut up!

Dief the Chief

John started most of his speeches the same way—by saying, "My fellow Canadians . . ." And many Canadians loved him. They loved his antics. They nicknamed him "Dief the Chief" and, in 1958, returned him to power with the largest majority in Canadian history.

John had a hard time working with other people. Even members of his own **cabinet** didn't like his "one-man rule." John hated to admit when he was wrong, and some of his best and most capable ministers resigned rather than submit to his domineering and overpowering personality. Yes, John's intolerance earned him lots of enemies! But it didn't deter him. He pressed forward, blasting away at everyone, always pointing out their mistakes.

He never backed down

Many thought John was crazy to be so obsessed with equal rights for all Canadians. But he refused to back down. He was the first—and remains the only—prime minister with roots that were neither entirely British nor French. Growing up with a German name, he knew the sting of prejudice. It made him fight to help those who also were treated unfairly. For instance, he was determined to see that Japanese Canadians and aboriginal people got the right to vote.

Even after it became clear that John would never be chief again, he refused to disappear into the background. He continued to be a thorn in the government's side right up to his death, a few months after his 13th election victory.

John knew the importance of standing up for one's beliefs. In a career that spanned almost four decades, he never backed down from fighting for issues he believed in, no matter how unpopular it made him. He was the prime minister who just would not quit, advising others that there was "no excuse for not standing for the things in which they believe."

John was the first PM to be passionate about equal rights for all Canadians.

On this topic, he said, "Being of mixed origin myself, I knew . . . in many parts of Canada, that citizenship depended upon surnames, or even upon blood counts.

"I made the initial determination to eliminate this feeling that being a Canadian was a matter of name and blood."

Politicians in the 1950s are supposed to be modest and restrained. That's not John's way. He has an intense, penetrating stare and a thunderous voice, and when he speaks, it is with great intensity and fire.

When John speaks in the House of Commons, he draws himself up to his full height—which at six feet two is pretty impressive. Placing one hand on his hip, he uses the other to thump the table or, most often, point directly at his target. His jowls shake and that pointing finger jabs at his victim with every word he bellows out.

1903

Doctors tell John's father that he should move his family west, saying the dry Prairie air will be good for his health. On August 15, the family boards a train heading to Saskatchewan, in what is then the Northwest Territories.

The train is filled with immigrant settlers just off the boat from Europe. Many are poorer than the Diefenbakers, but happily share what little they have. John and his brother sleep on a wooden shelf over the train's seats. The train is hot, damp, and uncomfortable. It constantly sways back and forth, sometimes violently.

Just a farmer's son

John's grandparents made the gruelling sea voyage from Germany to British North America (now Canada) in the 1850s. John's father, William Thomas Diefenbaker, was born in Ontario in 1868. William was a man with strong principles, and a great love of books and knowledge. When it came to politics, William started off as an enthusiastic supporter of **Sir Wilfrid Laurier** and the **Liberal party**. But once Laurier took a strong position against **conscription**, William switched his allegiance to the Conservative party.

Two future prime ministers

William worked as a teacher, a farmer, and a **civil servant**. While working as a teacher, he taught two future prime ministers—William Lyon Mackenzie King and his own son, John.

William met Mary Bannerman, his future wife, while he was teaching in the village of Underwood, Ontario. Mary's grandparents had come to Canada from Argyll, Scotland, in the mid-1820s. Her mother, Flora, had been born aboard a ship just as it docked in Newfoundland.

1895
John is born in Neustadt, Ontario.

1897
John's brother, Elmer, is born.

1900
Marie Curie discovers radiation (energy that's emitted as waves or moving particles).

1903
John's dad comes close to developing tuberculosis.

The family moves to Saskatchewan.

1905
Einstein publishes a paper proposing the equation $E=mc^2$.

Robert Koch wins the Nobel Peace Prize for discovering the cause of tuberculosis.

1908
John and his uncle get lost in a blizzard.

William and Mary were married in May 1894. John was born just over a year later, on September 18, 1895, in Neustadt, Ontario. Two years later, they had another son whom they named Elmer.

A few years later the family moved to Toronto, a city that, in those days, was mostly British. It wasn't a friendly place for non-British people, and the Diefenbaker boys' obviously German name made them easy targets for teasing.

Westward bound

In 1903, when John was eight, his dad was diagnosed as being on the verge of developing galloping consumption, now known as **tuberculosis** (TB). Doctors told William to move his family west, saying the dry Prairie air would be good for his health. All of their relatives were dead set against the idea—they thought the Diefenbaker family was going to the ends of the earth! But they went anyway. On August 15, they boarded a train heading for Saskatchewan, in what was then the Northwest Territories.

The Diefenbakers didn't have much money and the train's cars had no sleeping rooms, so Mary carefully packed bedrolls of quilts, pillows, blankets, and bagged lunches. But, would you believe it, William put it all on the wrong train—and that train left the station before their belongings could be retrieved! The family was forced to travel 2,800 kilometres without supplies.

An extremely difficult trip

The train was hot, damp, and uncomfortable. It constantly swayed back and forth, sometimes violently. The boys slept on wooden shelves over the train's seats. Each night, their parents tied them to the shelves so they wouldn't be flung across the car while they slept.

The train was filled with immigrant settlers, many just off the boat from Europe. A lot of them were poorer than the Diefenbakers, but they happily shared what little they had.

It was still an extremely difficult trip. Halfway there, John's father announced, "We're going back to Ontario!" John's mother calmly replied, "We started out and we're going on." When William insisted on turning back, she responded, "If you do leave, the rest of us will carry on, and you'll come out sooner or later." William stayed.

After a short rest in Rosthern, Northwest Territories (now Saskatchewan), the family boarded a double-box wagon for the Tiefengrund schoolhouse, near Fort Carlton. This would be William's next teaching position and their new home. The roads were narrow, potholed, dirt trails. As you can imagine, it was a long and bumpy ride!

When John was a kid, tuberculosis was a killer disease. People who got it developed a terrible cough, and often looked as though the disease was consuming them from inside. That's why it used to be called "the Consumption."

John's father's teaching position is in a tiny one-room schoolhouse at the end of a narrow, potholed, dirt trail. The family's new home is attached to the same building.

The Diefenbakers' door is always open. Their home quickly becomes a community centre and meeting place. It's also a natural stopping place for travellers. Aboriginals, salesmen, school inspectors, and members of the Northwest Mounted Police all stop by to sample Mary's cooking.

Their home was three rooms and a kitchen attached to the back of a one-room schoolhouse. The Diefenbaker home served as a community centre and meeting place. It was also a natural stopping place for travellers. The Diefenbakers' door was always open. Natives, salesmen, school inspectors, and members of the **Northwest Mounted Police** all stopped by to sample Mary's cooking.

William strongly believed in giving to all who were in need, no matter the cost. He told his boys that, in giving, one was bound to make a mistake now and then, but that he would sooner make the mistake of giving than of not giving. These lessons stayed with John all his life.

The best shot in the West

The schoolhouse was only a few kilometres from Duck Lake, site of the first battle of the 1885 **Northwest Rebellion**. John was both fascinated and frightened when **Gabriel Dumont**, the famous **Métis** war general, came to their house. Dumont was a big bear of a man. It was said that he spoke six languages, that he'd led the biggest buffalo hunts ever, and that he was the best shot in the West!

William tried his hand at farming. He bought a homestead about 50 kilometres southeast of Carlton, Saskatchewan. John and Elmer helped their father clear the land and build a house. It was there that John announced he would one day be prime minister. His mom, an ever-practical woman, pointed out the impossibility of a boy from the Prairies reaching that position, but John would not be swayed.

A magical place

For a couple of young boys, the Prairies of the early 1900s was a magical place. There were jackrabbits and wildfowl in abundance and at night the skies were ablaze with northern lights, seemingly dancing to the cries of the coyotes. But it was also harsh. Summers were hot. Wild fires, swarming bugs, and terrible summer storms were always just over the horizon. Winters were absolutely frigid! Much too cold for the tiny, hastily built shacks the settlers lived in. Blizzards would hit without warning, often taking the lives of unsuspecting travellers.

One winter, the temperature never made it above -15°C for a whole month and often fell to -50°C at night. Another winter, in 1908, John and his uncle got lost in a blizzard. They spent the night stuck in a snowdrift, huddling together and fighting to stay awake because falling asleep would have meant certain death.

Before Saskatchewan joined Confederation, in 1905, it belonged to a territory called "Rupert's Land." Rupert's Land was owned by the Hudson's Bay Company, which we now know as "The Bay."

The Prairies are a magical place, with jackrabbits and wildfowl in abundance and night skies ablaze with northern lights. But life here is harsh. Summers are unbelievably hot, with wild fires, swarming bugs, and terrible storms.

In winter, temperatures might not make it above -15°C for a whole month, and commonly fall to -50°C at night. Blizzards hit without warning, often taking the lives of unsuspecting travellers. On one occasion, John and his uncle get lost in such a blizzard. They spend all night stuck in a snowdrift, huddling together and fighting to stay awake because falling asleep would mean certain death.

1910

While peddling newspapers near the train station, John marches up to Prime Minister Wilfrid Laurier to sell him a paper. Transaction complete, Laurier tries to engage John in small talk.

After a short chat, John brushes off Sir Wilfrid, saying "Sorry, Prime Minister, I can't waste any more time on you. I've got work to do!" This brief encounter inspires young John to believe "that no matter his upbringing, anyone can rise to any position in this country."

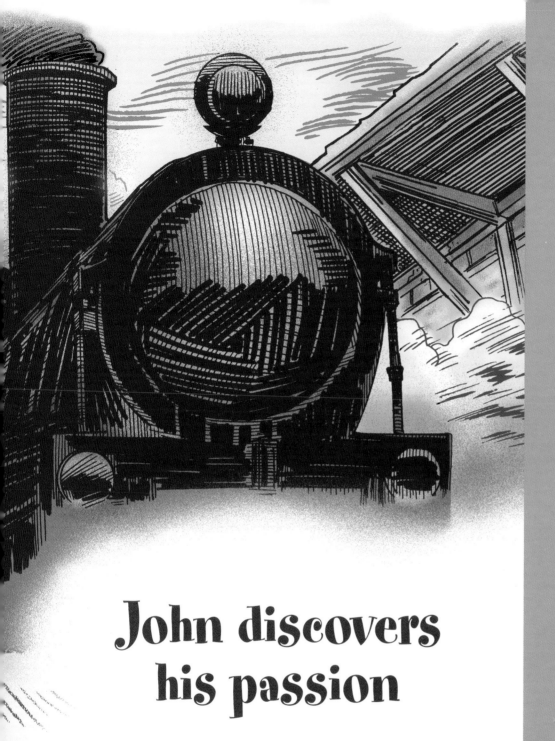

John discovers his passion

John's interest in politics was inherited from his father. While attending teacher's college in Ottawa, William had practically lived in the **visitors' gallery** of the **House of Commons**. **Sir John A. Macdonald**, Canada's first prime minister, was in his last year of office and the workings of the House fascinated William. "The House of Commons lived for him," recalled John, "and it lived for me when I heard him recount the events he had witnessed."

1910
John's family moves to Saskatoon.

Newspaper vendor John has a chat with Prime Minister Laurier.

1914
World War I begins on August 1. Seventy Canadian soldiers will receive the Victoria Cross (see right) for bravery in battle.

The University of Saskatchewan's newspaper predicts John will be Opposition leader by 1955. It's off by one year.

1915
John graduates from university.

1916
John completes his master's degree.

He joins the 105th Saskatoon Fusiliers, but is injured and discharged.

1917
The National Hockey League (NHL) is created.

1918
World War I ends.

All Canadian women over the age of 21 are allowed to vote in federal elections.

1919
John is called to the bar of Saskatchewan.

Inspiration takes hold

John's interest in politics grew. He was shy and found it hard to speak to strangers, especially girls. But when inspiration took hold, he could become very passionate. Like the night when he was 13 years old—he was at a Farmers' Institute meeting and became angry over the problems that the farmers faced. They were complaining about difficulties with the faulty equipment they were sold, and their struggles to sell their wheat at a fair price. Impulsively, John stood up and shouted, "This thing is wrong and someday I'm going to do my part to put an end to this." People could hardly believe their ears. The audience roared with applause.

Dief meets Laurier

In 1910, Mary decided her boys needed a city education, so they packed up and moved to Saskatoon. John was now 15 years old and he got a job to save for school. He sold three newspapers, the *Saskatoon Phoenix*, the *Winnipeg Tribune*, and the *Calgary Eye Opener*, all at the same time. One day, while peddling his papers near the train station, John spotted Prime Minister Wilfrid Laurier standing by his private train car. John marched right up to him and offered him a paper. Laurier paid John a quarter—that was five times more than the actual cost of the paper! Laurier and John talked about Canada. But John, having to get back to work said, "Sorry, Prime Minister, I can't waste any more time on you. I've got work to do." Later that same day, as Laurier laid the cornerstone of the University of Saskatchewan, he included John's remarks in his speech.

John studied at the University of Saskatchewan. On his very first day at university, he landed—splash—in the fountain! Not of his own accord, mind you. No, he was heaved into the fancy fountain by some excited students. He was an innocent victim of a practical joke.

Run-ins with the police

John worked hard to pay his university fees, especially during the summers. One summer, John and a classmate peddled Bibles and law books by bicycle, door to door, farm to farm, across Saskatchewan. Poor John had run-ins with the police twice that summer! First, he was arrested in Hanley for selling without a licence (the licence was back at the office with his employer). Then, in Outlook, the police picked him up because they thought he was a vagrant.

But John's great passion was politics. While at university, he mastered the rules of Parliament and the art of debate. In his last year, he was elected leader of the Opposition party in the university's **mock parliament**. The university's newspaper, the *Sheaf*, predicted he'd be leader of Canada's official Opposition by 1955. They were off by only one year!

Prime Minister Laurier paid John 25¢ for a 5¢ newspaper—five times the cost! Not a bad tip, eh?

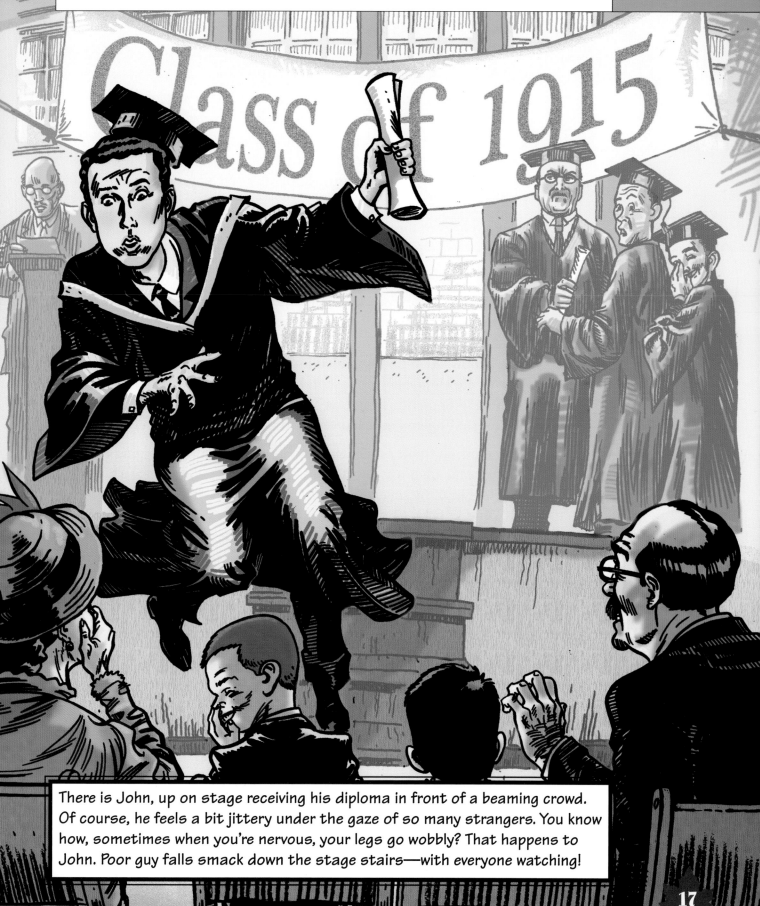

John's graduation is especially memorable—but not in a way that anyone would enjoy! First, his name is left off of the graduation program. Once that error is corrected, everyone heaves a sigh of relief. But more is to come . . .

There is John, up on stage receiving his diploma in front of a beaming crowd. Of course, he feels a bit jittery under the gaze of so many strangers. You know how, sometimes when you're nervous, your legs go wobbly? That happens to John. Poor guy falls smack down the stage stairs—with everyone watching!

John's graduation, in May 1915, was especially memorable and not in a way that he enjoyed! The first shock came when his name was left off the graduation program. John, Elmer, and their father feared he would not be graduating after all! Only his mother remained calm. Of course, it turned out to be a big mistake and was soon corrected. Everyone heaved a sigh of relief.

Finally, everything seemed to be going well. There was John, up on stage receiving his diploma in front of a beaming crowd. Of course, he felt a bit jittery under the gaze of so many strangers, but what could go wrong? Well, you know how sometimes when you're nervous your legs go wobbly? That happened to John. Poor guy fell smack down the stage stairs—with everyone watching!

That did not put John off university life, though. In 1916, he completed a Master of Arts degree in economics and political science.

Going to war

By now, **World War I** had been raging across Europe for almost two years. Like many young men, John desperately wanted to take part. While still working on his Master of Arts, he volunteered for overseas service. He didn't know when he'd be called for duty so he enrolled in the College of Law at the University of Saskatchewan. Soon after beginning his law training in September, he was standing on the deck of the SS *Lapland*, heading to England as a lieutenant in the 105th Saskatoon Fusiliers.

John enjoyed military life, working long hours, often digging trenches. But his war career was short-lived. One day, someone threw a heavy digging tool into the seven-foot trench he was working in. It struck him on the spine, knocking him down. He was bleeding heavily and it only began to ease after a few days. It started up again, but this time he was bleeding from the mouth. John was declared medically unfit to serve. He was discharged and shipped home to Canada.

His military career over, he returned to Saskatoon to finish his law training. He was called to the bar of Saskatchewan in 1919.

John says he left the army because he got hit by a shovel—but that's not what the army says!

The army refused to give him a pension, saying he was discharged because of "general weakness," not due to any physical injuries.

The many casualties of war

War is bloody, messy, and dangerous. Those who have managed to survive it will tell you that they'd never want to go through it again. War changes people, and can leave them with deep scars, both physically and emotionally. And, of course, many who go off to fight don't come back alive.

During the early years of Canada, war was often fought between small groups of soldiers, usually no more than a couple hundred men on each side. Battles would last a few hours at most, and while soldiers could be killed or injured, most would emerge unscathed. In the 18th and 19th centuries, armies usually lost more men to disease than to attacks by the enemy.

World War I (1914–1918) saw a huge change in how a war was fought, and what it did to soldiers. When that war began, it was believed that the fighting would be over in a few weeks, and there would be few casualties on either side. But the war was fought to a standstill. As both sides hunkered down into trenches, they started to invent new ways to kill and maim each other. It was during this conflict that machine guns and giant artillery pieces were made lethally effective—these weapons could literally tear apart a human being. Even worse was the introduction of poison gas—combinations of chemicals that created toxic clouds over the battlefield. These gases could destroy your lungs from the inside out.

Thousands of people are killed or maimed by land mines every year

These new weapons were capable of a destruction never experienced before. Tens of thousands of soldiers could be killed in a single day of fighting. World War I also saw a new kind of injury: shell shock. Many soldiers could not endure the horrors of war, or seeing their friends die, and this caused them to develop psychological illnesses. Some could not eat or sleep, others had terrible nightmares or became hysterical. Most could never return to duty and were traumatized by their experiences for years afterward.

Although people were horrified by the death and destruction caused by World War I, the years since have seen weapons become even more deadly. And wars today often kill far more civilians than soldiers. Sometimes this is done deliberately. Or sometimes civilians caught in the crossfire are considered "collateral damage."

Over the last 50 years, Canadian soldiers have acted as peacekeepers around the world to limit the damage caused by warfare and its weapons. In recent years, Canadians have led the way in getting most of the world to ban the use of land mines. A land mine is a type of bomb that's buried in the ground and explodes when somebody walks or drives over it. Armies often plant thousands of land mines in the ground, but once the fighting is over, nobody retrieves them. These weapons often kill or maim people years after a war has ended, and remain a serious problem in many countries.

For more information about war casualties, visit our website at www.jackfruitpress.com.

1919

John's first real experience with the law is delivering papers to the district court. John is proud of himself but also quite nervous. It shows.

Making his way to the judge's desk, John accidentally steps into a small wire garbage can. Since John's foot is firmly wedged, it takes several minutes to remove it. Meanwhile, the judge watches and waits.

Passing the bar

John became a lawyer at the age of 24. This was the first step toward his dream of becoming prime minister. He chose to set up an office in the village of Wakaw, Saskatchewan. Wakaw had a population of 600 people, with several thousand others living within 30 kilometres of the town. It was close enough to Saskatoon to visit his parents on weekends, and had a Baptist church. It seemed ideal. But there was one catch—there were no empty offices!

First experience with the law

This did not, of course, stop John. He found a small lot he could build on and, with a loan from the North American Lumber Company and the help of a French-Canadian carpenter, built his own office.

John's first experience with the law was delivering papers to District Court Judge E. A. C. McLorg. While nervously making his way to the judge's desk, John stepped into a small wire garbage can. His foot firmly wedged, it took several minutes to physically remove it. The judge just watched and waited. Just imagine how embarrassing that was for John!

1919
John becomes a lawyer and sets up an office in Wakaw, Saskatchewan.

The Winnipeg General Strike takes place from May 15 to June 26.

John wins his first case. He then takes on 62 more trials in this same year.

1920
Jazz becomes a popular form of music in North America.

1921
Agnes Macphail becomes the first woman elected to Parliament.

The local Liberal party tries repeatedly to recruit John. He keeps refusing to join.

1922
Fascist leader Benito Mussolini is appointed prime minister of Italy.

1923
Adolf Hitler tries but fails to form a new government in Germany.

John's first client was his brother, Elmer. Always a tease, Elmer asked John for some legal advice, then gave him a dollar, saying the dollar was worth more than any advice John could give him! Elmer was John's best friend and biggest supporter, but from their letters you could see that Elmer loved to give John a hard time.

John wins his first case

John's first real case was for a local Ukrainian farmer named John Chernyski. One night at dusk, Chernyski had shot his neighbour, claiming he'd mistaken him for a coyote. Even though the man swore it was an accident and had run five kilometres to fetch the doctor, he was charged with **criminal negligence**. It was well known that he hated his neighbour.

John convinced the jury that it had been light enough that night for a man to see something, but dark enough for him to be easily mistaken. The judge and jury believed John's version of the events and Chernyski was not jailed. John was overjoyed—he'd won his very first case. In that first year, he took on 62 trials, winning about half of them.

As a lawyer and later as prime minister, John wrestled with the concept of the death penalty. Always against the taking of a human life, John was horrified when one of his clients, convicted of killing his girlfriend, was proven innocent only a few months after being hanged.

Friends and enemies

John never charged a Métis or aboriginal for his legal advice. "I was distressed by the unbelievable poverty and the injustice done them," said John. His generosity made him an almost mythical figure to the First Nations people.

First Nations author **Maria Campbell** wrote, "He was colourful, dashing, and exciting and he would represent anyone, rich or poor, red or white. If they had a case and no money, he would help…Our people would come for miles in rain or snow to watch him. Then they would go home and repeat what had happened, and by the second repetition John was 10 feet taller."

But John was also making enemies. By 1921, he had won some high-profile cases and was making a name for himself. The local Liberal party, seeing his potential as a strong politician, asked him to join them. John refused—but they persisted. They even secretly elected him party secretary and slipped into his office, leaving their books on his desk. He was furious and marched them right back. This was the beginning of a life-long clash between John and the local Liberals.

John was famous for his concern about the rights of common folks. He once said, "As long as there's a drop of blood in my body, they won't stop me from talking about freedom."

Defending human rights all over the world

Growing up on the vast plains of Saskatchewan, John came to see himself as something of an outsider in this country. He did not have an English or French last name like most people—and in the Canada of that era, this meant that you were sometimes considered not a real citizen of this country. John was determined to break through this barrier, even though he was an underdog.

John's outsider status made him want to stand up and protect other underdogs—people who were being treated unfairly or who were denied their rights. You could see this even when John was a lawyer. He took on cases that other lawyers did not want, because the client was too poor or had little chance of winning. These were people like Nadia Bajer, a single mother who was falsely accused of killing her own baby, or

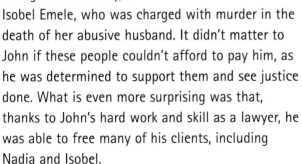

Nelson Mandela, imprisoned for opposing the racist policies that Diefenbaker denounced

Isobel Emele, who was charged with murder in the death of her abusive husband. It didn't matter to John if these people couldn't afford to pay him, as he was determined to support them and see justice done. What is even more surprising was that, thanks to John's hard work and skill as a lawyer, he was able to free many of his clients, including Nadia and Isobel.

John continued to fight for the underdog when he was elected as a **member of Parliament**. In 1942, the Canadian government decided that all people of Japanese ancestry would be taken away from their homes and forced to live in prison camps. The government insisted it had to do this because Canada was at war with Japan, and that some Japanese people might act as spies. But Diefenbaker was one of the very few politicians who argued against this. He later wrote, "to take a whole people and condemn them as wrongdoers because of race was something I could not accept."

During the war, John spent much of his time in Ottawa, trying to prevent the government from harassing the Japanese, or religious groups like the Jehovah's Witnesses, who did not want to join the army.

John's ideals did not leave him when he became prime minister either. In fact, he was able to achieve one of his biggest goals—a **Bill of Rights** for all Canadians. On the world stage, he took the lead in denouncing the racist policies of South Africa when it would have been very easy for him and other Canadians just to ignore what was happening half a world away. He did it because he believed that you had to stand up and protect those who needed help—and if they were the underdog, you had to help even more.

For more information about human rights, visit our website at www.jackfruitpress.com.

1934

Some achievements don't come easy, such as John's rise to leadership. He keeps trying, trying, and trying to get elected.

At one point, the Saskatchewan Conservatives are so poor they can't afford to cover the election costs of their candidates. John, out of his own pocket, puts up the money for himself and 22 other candidates to run. Every single candidate loses! John's zest for politics is wavering.

Try, try, and try again

Notable achievements rarely come easy. Often, the things we desire most are the hardest to reach. This was how it was with John and politics. The year after he opened his office in Wakaw, he ran for village council and won. But it would be his last political victory for many, many years.

John opened a law practice in Prince Albert in 1924 but faithfully returned to Saskatoon to visit his parents every weekend. On his travels, he met a lively schoolteacher named **Edna Mae Brower**. Edna was soon John's sweetheart. Friends weren't sure how two such opposites could be happy together—John was so quiet and Edna was so outgoing!

"It is my destiny"

Edna was fascinated by John and by his dream of becoming prime minister of Canada. He told her that it was "more than a goal—it is my destiny."

By 1925, he was ready to try his hand at federal politics. His opponents spread horrible and untrue rumours suggesting that John was associated with the German forces during World War I. This was because of his German name. It didn't help that the Conservatives—the party he was running for—planned to make changes to the Crow's Nest Pass freight rate. This was a very important program that helped farmers pay to ship their grain to West Coast ports. John didn't stand a chance! Not surprisingly, he lost.

John and Edna were married in 1929, the same year he ran for the provincial Conservatives in Arm River against one of his old Liberal

1924
John starts a law practice in Prince Albert.

1925
John runs for federal office and loses.

1929
John marries Edna Mae Brower.

The stock market collapses on October 29, marking the start of the Great Depression.

1930
John is named King's Counsel in the New Year's honours list.

Cairine Wilson becomes Canada's first female appointed senator.

A US astronomer discovers Pluto, the ninth planet from the sun.

1935
Men from BC work camps march on Parliament Hill, looking for proper wages.

1939
World War II begins.

1940
John wins his first federal election. He and Edna move to Ottawa.

enemies, T. C. Davis. John lost by only a few hundred votes. Later, he was elected vice-president of the Saskatchewan provincial Conservatives. Later still, he ran for mayor of Prince Albert, losing again, but this time by only 20 votes.

The Great Depression

Luckily, John had his law career to fall back on; Canada was quickly slipping into a deep **economic depression**. Thousands of young men were **riding the rods**—travelling across the country by train—desperately looking for work. Many ended up in government-run work camps making as little as 20¢ a day for eight hours of hard labour. In 1935, out of desperation, many men from the work camps in British Columbia decided to march to Parliament Hill to force the government to pay them proper wages. But the government saw to it that their "On-to-Ottawa Trek" never reached its destination.

John kept trying to get elected. At this time, the Saskatchewan Conservatives were so poor they couldn't afford to help candidates cover their election costs. John, out of his own pocket, put up the money for himself and 22 other candidates to run. Every single candidate lost! John's zest for politics was wavering.

Sick and tired of losing

The last few years had been very tough at home. Edna had not been well. She had been in and out of hospital fighting depression and insomnia (an inability to sleep). Edna was exhausted. She had changed from being outgoing to not wanting to be around people at all.

The stress of caring for Edna and maintaining a law office during what seemed like constant campaigning was taking its toll on John. He'd lost five times and was sick and tired of it!

In 1939, he reluctantly agreed to attend the federal Conservatives' Lake Centre nomination meeting in Imperial, Saskatchewan. At first, he let his name stand as a candidate, then changed his mind and withdrew it. John and Edna left the meeting and were already in their car when an old friend, Ed Topping, came running out, urging John to come back to the meeting. In John's absence, the delegates had ignored his withdrawal and elected him anyway. This show of support pleased him and sparked his interest in politics again.

With Edna at his side, John packed 57 meetings and did two 15-minute radio shows every week for five weeks. He called for a fair, stable, predictable price for wheat and the farmers listened. On March 26, 1940, it happened. John won! It had taken 15 years and six elections, but John was finally going to Ottawa!

During the Great Depression, some people couldn't afford gas, so they pulled their cars with horses. These contraptions were called "Bennett buggies," after Richard Bennett, Canada's prime minister at the time.

The Great Depression in the Prairies

The Dirty '30s were a time of great hardship, especially on the Prairies. Not only were people saddled with a worldwide economic depression, but also one of the worse droughts in Canadian history.

Wanna know why the '30s were so "dirty" in the first place? Dust storms, caused by a massive drought and years of poor agricultural techniques, sent dry topsoil blowing across the Prairies, creating what was called a "dust bowl." People reported that the dust storms turned the skies black in the middle of the afternoon. In addition to the drifting topsoil, grasshoppers, weeds, and wheat rust devastated crops and forced two-thirds of the rural population to seek government help.

In the early part of the 1900s, Canada had the fastest growing economy in the world. The country's prosperity was largely due to being a net exporter of wheat. But by 1937, Saskatchewan's wheat yield fell from about six bushels per hectare to 1.08 bushels. Farmers still had trouble selling their limited crops, however, as many countries could not afford to import wheat anyway due to their own economic difficulties during the Depression.

Starvation was a real threat for a great number of Canadian families—some even resorted to hunting rodents! Thousands of unemployed workers relied on the free food provided by soup kitchens, or "rode the rods" looking for work.

In Western Canada, new political parties formed during the Depression, including the Social Credit Party of Canada and the Co-operative Commonwealth Federation (CCF). These parties offered different economic reforms to help solve the problems of the Depression, and the CCF, in particular, had a great impact on Canadian politics. For instance, the CCF's goal of creating a welfare state where unemployment insurance, workers' compensation, children's allowances, universal pensions, and health insurance would become foundations of Canadian society. In 1944, the CCF formed the provincial government of Saskatchewan—the first socialist government in North America. Its leader, Tommy Douglas, initiated universal health care in Saskatchewan and, in the 1960s, Prime Minister Lester B. Pearson made this a national policy.

The Depression lasted until 1939, when World War II started. The war created a demand for materials, and many unemployed people enlisted in the military. Economic conditions improved all over the world, particularly in the United States, creating a market for Canadian wheat and other commodities once again.

The 1930s were a time of great social upheaval

For more information about the labour movement, visit our website at www.jackfruitpress.com.

1940

John loves the House of Commons, but doesn't fit in. He's different—a westerner who speaks with passion and fire while other politicians speak coolly and with far less emotion.

His thunderous voice and sometimes theatrical antics get him noticed. He stands tall, his hand on his hip, his finger stabbing at his target, driving home each word. When he finishes, he often tosses his papers into the air, letting them fall to the floor.

In the House at last

In early 1940, John started his parliamentary career in Ottawa. He loved the House of Commons, but he didn't fit in. He was different—a westerner who spoke with passion and fire when other politicians spoke coolly and with far less emotion. He was a man of the people who pushed for a new vision of Canada—"One Canada"—where everyone, no matter their race, heritage, or economic standing, had the same rights. This was a brand new idea to many in Ottawa who saw no need to give rights to **First Nations peoples** or recent immigrants.

Life inside the House

John was quick to laugh. His thunderous voice and sometimes childish antics were getting him noticed. He'd stand tall, his hand on his hips, his finger stabbing at his target, driving home each word. When he finished speaking he'd often toss his papers into the air, letting them fall to the floor.

His wife, Edna, spent her afternoons in the visitors' gallery of the House of Commons watching him give speeches and debate with other members of Parliament. When John was too busy to go to the House himself, Edna would report to John what she had seen and heard.

John fought the government on many points—conscription, the treatment of **Jehovah's Witnesses**, and the wartime oppression of Japanese Canadians. His life had become so busy by now that he had to miss his parents' fiftieth wedding anniversary celebration. His mother was very upset!

1940
John starts his parliamentary career.

1945
World War II ends.

John represents Canada in the founding of the United Nations.

John's father dies on February 12.

All final appeals are now handled by the Supreme Court of Canada.

1950
The Korean War begins.

1951
Edna dies of leukemia on February 7.

John wins a famous case defending Alfred John Atherton in the deaths of 21 people.

1953
John marries Olive Freeman Palmer.

John wins another election in a different riding.

The Korean War ends.

1956
John becomes leader of the Progressive Conservative Party of Canada.

side was so that no matter what they might find in Korea, they'd always be able to say, 'Well, we had it worse in Canada.'" The courtroom was stunned. An argument broke out between John and the Crown prosecutor, a retired army colonel from World War I. The Crown prosecutor, in his rage, said, "I want to make it clear that in this case we're not concerned about the death of a few privates going to Korea." He, of course, meant that the case against Atherton was for the death of the four crew members, not the soldiers, but John quickly jumped on his mistake. He said, "You are not concerned about the killing of a few privates? Oh, Colonel!" It was the boost that John needed. The jury acquitted Atherton. Sadly, Edna didn't live to hear the verdict.

Little time to mourn

When Edna died on February 7, 1952, John was heartbroken. The First Baptist church, in Saskatoon, overflowed with mourners.

While John mourned, the Liberals plotted his demise. In 1952, they reorganized the **ridings** in Saskatchewan; his riding of Lake Centre was eliminated. This meant that John had no place to run. He wondered if he should retire from politics. He loved practising law and had received some job offers from law firms in Ontario. But John decided that if the Liberals were determined to get rid of him, he was determined to stay and fight. The only question he had was "where was I to fight?"

John went on a fishing trip with his brother, Elmer, and two politicians from rival parties. You see, even some Saskatchewan Liberals and Social Credit members didn't want to see John retire from politics. John loved to fish and once he was on the lake, and relaxed, they hit him with a proposal. Would he run in Prince Albert? Reluctantly, he agreed, saying the **gerrymandering** (this is what you call it when someone divides a place into election districts in a way that gives an unfair advantage to one political party) of his riding had made him angry and even more determined to win. And win he did! He put his heart and soul into the 1953 election and won by 3,001 votes.

But without Edna, John was lost. Friends tried to console him by inviting him to various social functions around Ottawa. But John's heart was not in it. Not long after that, John ran into **Olive Freeman Palmer**, whom he had first met as a young man on his return from the war in 1917. She was now a senior civil servant with the Ontario Department of Education in Toronto and a widow with a teenage daughter named **Carolyn Palmer**. He dated her in secret, and only told his closest friends about her after they were married!

Gerrymandering? There's another new word to add to your growing list of political tricks!

During this time, John kept plugging away, unwavering in his quest for the position of prime minister. He ran twice for the leadership of the federal Conservatives, but lost. Then, in December 1956, with only a few months until the next election, Conservative party leader **George Drew** became ill. The party needed a leader, fast! John was now a proven vote-getter because of the Canoe River case, so they decided to give him a chance. At the age of 61, John finally became leader of the Conservative party, just one step away from his ultimate goal—becoming prime minister of Canada!

John's Liberal opponents have eliminated his riding, leaving him no place to run for office. To convince him to stay in the fight, John's brother invites him to go fishing with two politicians from rival parties.

1952

The three men know that John loves to fish. Once he's on the lake, and relaxed, they hit him with a proposal. Would he run in Prince Albert? Reluctantly, John agrees, saying the gerrymandering of his riding has made him angry and even more determined to win. Putting his heart and soul into the 1953 election, he wins by 3,001 votes.

1957

Being prime minister is hard work. John wonders how other prime ministers managed to take time off for holidays. For John, 17-hour days are normal.

John tries to make himself available to everyone as much as possible. Even a group of students touring Parliament Hill can find themselves in John's office, where he talks with them about being the prime minister. Still, he can't please everybody. He's criticized for his decision-making skills—some people complain he delays everything, while others complain he makes decisions too quickly!

Finally in charge of the country

John shone as **Opposition leader**. He took every opportunity to get under Prime Minister **Louis St. Laurent**'s skin. He refused to move to **Stornoway**, the official home of the Opposition leader, believing he would soon be prime minister. And he was right.

By now the Liberal party had been in power for over 22 years, and the Canadian people were looking for change. Everyone started to look at Diefenbaker, who now had the nickname "Dief the Chief." They thought he would bring new and fresh ideas to the country.

John becomes prime minister

John went out on the campaign trail, promising to reduce taxes, increase old-age pensions, and bring roads and other development to northern Canada. On June 10, 1957, the Conservatives took power. They won with a small majority, 112 seats to the Liberals' 105.

John was thrilled, and immediately went to visit his ailing mother in a Saskatoon hospital. "This is quite a thing, isn't it?" she said calmly. Then she reminded him not to "forget the poor and the afflicted. Do the best you can for as long as you can." It was not quite the reaction he had hoped for! He had expected her to be really excited for him.

1957
The Conservatives win the federal election and John becomes prime minister.

John appoints Ellen Louks Fairclough as Canada's first female federal cabinet minister.

The USSR launches the first two earth satellites, Sputnik I and II.

1958
John introduces legislation to protect the Sable Island ponies.

John appoints James Gladstone, a native Canadian, to the Senate.

Canada's Bill of Rights is introduced.

The St. Lawrence Seaway opens.

Meanwhile, John took up his duties as prime minister. His first cabinet included **Ellen Louks Fairclough** as secretary of state. She was Canada's first female federal cabinet minister.

The largest majority in Canada's history

John was happy to be prime minister but it was difficult trying to get things done with such a slim majority. To pass anything, he needed 21 opposition MPs to vote with him. It was a major pain. John had a very strong feeling that, if he called another election, he would likely win most of the seats. Again he was right. Only one year later, John's government won the largest majority in the history of Canada. It was the highest voter turnout for any federal election in Canadian history, with 79.4 per cent of people voting. John's plans to open up the North convinced 90 per cent of Yukoners to cast their votes.

Being prime minister was hard work. John couldn't imagine how other prime ministers had managed to take time off for holidays. For John, 17-hour days were normal. He would start each morning at 5:30, snacking on half a grapefruit or an orange and a cup of coffee. He dictated letters and memos for an hour, went for a walk, then returned home to join Olive for breakfast. He was at his office by 8 a.m.

John tried to make himself available to everyone as much as possible—from the man on the street to powerful industrialists. Even a group of students touring Parliament Hill could find themselves in John's office, where he would talk with them about being the prime minister. Still, he couldn't please everybody. He was criticized for his decision-making skills—some people complained he delayed everything, while others complained that he decided things too quickly!

The Sable Island ponies

John's love of animals was tested in 1958, when the **Crown Assets Disposal Corporation** made a deplorable decision. Two hundred and fifty ponies on Sable Island (a small island 300 kilometres southeast of Halifax, Nova Scotia) were declared surplus. Canadians couldn't imagine how a part of their natural heritage could be destroyed and, as rumour had it, turned into dog food!

The ponies (actually wild horses) had lived freely on the island for at least 200 years. Some were descendants of horses

The Cold War and the Cuban missile crisis

From the 1940s to the 1990s, the threat of a massive war was on the minds of nearly everyone. People had already experienced two world wars, but with the invention of nuclear weapons it seemed that if it happened again there would be nothing left of the earth.

On one side of this conflict were the nations of Western Europe and North America, including Canada, the United States, France, and Great Britain. All these nations were capitalist. On the opposite side was a group that included the Soviet Union (now known as Russia) and other **communist** nations. For various reasons, both sides loathed and distrusted each other, but because they both possessed huge amounts of **weapons of mass destruction**, neither wanted to be the one that would start a new war. This standoff came to be called the **Cold War**. This war involved few major confrontations but included a lot of spying and involvement in smaller conflicts. Weapon stockpiling was viewed as a deterrent to actual armed conflict. Various treaties were signed to control the proliferation of nuclear weapons. They included the 1968 Non-Proliferation Treaty (NPT), the Strategic Arms Limitation treaties SALT I (1972) and SALT II (1979), the 1972 Anti-Ballistic Missile (ABM) Treaty, and the Comprehensive Test Ban Treaty (CTBT) of the early 1990s.

John Diefenbaker became prime minister during one of the most difficult periods of the Cold War, when there was a lot of tension between the United States and the Soviet Union. John was very much opposed to communism, but was not fond of the United States either because he had a terrible relationship with US president **John F. Kennedy**. The two men just did not get along with each other, getting upset over the tiniest things.

On October 14, 1962, US spy planes discovered that the Soviet Union was secretly building nuclear missile launching sites on the island of Cuba, which lies just south of Florida. If the Soviets were to place nuclear missiles there, it would mean that all of North America would be in extreme danger. President Kennedy acted quickly—on October 22, he announced the discovery of these missile sites and set up a naval blockade around Cuba to prevent anyone from bringing more military equipment to the island. A fleet of Soviet ships was heading there at this time, and many people feared that if they tried to break through the US blockade, it would start a third world war. The crisis lasted until October 28, when a deal was made in which the Soviets agreed to remove all nuclear weapons from Cuba, while the United States withdrew missiles it had set up in Turkey. It would be the scariest moment in the Cold War, and afterward many Canadians would come to believe that nuclear missiles were so dangerous that efforts should be made to limit their spread and use.

For more information about the Cold War, visit our website at www.jackfruitpress.com.

37

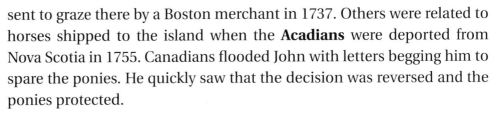

sent to graze there by a Boston merchant in 1737. Others were related to horses shipped to the island when the **Acadians** were deported from Nova Scotia in 1755. Canadians flooded John with letters begging him to spare the ponies. He quickly saw that the decision was reversed and the ponies protected.

He also kept his campaign promises to Canada's First Nations peoples—first, in 1958, by appointing **James Gladstone**, from the **Blood Reserve** in Alberta, to the Senate, then by securing the vote for all aboriginal Canadians two years later.

John's government achieved many other things during his roughly six-year reign, including doubling the payouts for pensions and employment insurance and opening up the North. But John wrote later that his biggest accomplishment was the Bill of Rights, which set out to protect the **civil liberties** of all Canadians. John had been discriminated against just because his last name was German, and he did not want future generations of Canadians to have to go through the same kind of prejudice that he had faced.

The beginning of the end

Despite this important accomplishment, the first signs of John's downfall were starting to emerge. The small-town lawyer had always seen himself as a fighter for the little guy, and he always believed he had many enemies. In fact, he saw anyone who did not totally support him as his enemy, and he would treat them with contempt and disdain.

Before he became prime minister, John was good friends with the newspaper and television reporters who covered politics in Ottawa. But once he was in power, Diefenbaker changed this relationship—he demanded the media give him their reverence and loyalty. If a reporter called him by his first name, Diefenbaker would take him aside and yell at him for hours, demanding that he refer to him only as "Prime Minister."

In response, the media were all too willing to point out the problems of the Conservative government, including Canada's high rate of **unemployment**, **budget deficits** year after year, the cancellation of the **Avro Arrow**, and how the Canadian dollar was worth only 92.5¢ compared to the US dollar. The Liberal party under **Lester Pearson** mocked John for the falling dollar by printing phony dollar bills that people called "Diefenbucks."

Here's what part of the Bill of Rights says:

"I am a Canadian, a free Canadian, free to speak without fear, free to worship God in my own way, free to stand for what I think is right, free to oppose what I believe is wrong, free to choose those who shall govern my country."

1958

Summoned to Ottawa to meet with the prime minister, Crawford Gordon, the head of A. V. Roe, suspects the Arrow project will be scrapped. Typically, he shows up with a cigar in his mouth and smelling of Scotch. He is in no mood to talk calmly.

Pounding on the prime minister's desk, Gordon demands that the Arrow not be scrapped. John warns him that if he doesn't lower his voice and stop the pounding, he'll be forcibly removed. Gordon responds by turning and stomping out of the PM's office with his trench coat flaring behind him like a cape. His meeting with John has lasted less than 20 minutes. The Arrow's fate is sealed.

Chief no more

The 1962 federal election was the beginning of the end for John Diefenbaker. He went into the campaign thinking he would easily win, but the result was a major blow to the Conservatives. They lost nearly half their seats, leaving them again with a minority government.

People around the prime minister knew something was wrong with him. Even at the best of times John could be mean and petty, but the pressure of being PM was making him snap. He thought there was a big conspiracy against him. He felt that not only were the Liberals trying to topple him from power, but also other Conservative party members, big business, the media, and the United States. Those around him would later write that John was "excited to a disturbing degree," "on the verge of exhaustion," "closer to hysteria than I have see him," and a "raging lunatic."

"It is time you went"

The big issue after the 1962 election was whether or not Canada would use **nuclear warheads** on the **Bomarc missiles** they had ordered from the United States. Many Canadians were opposed to having any kind of nuclear weapons, and they were sending thousands of letters to the prime minister asking him not to accept

1958
John cancels production of the Avro Arrow jet fighter.

1961
John's mother dies.

John attends the Commonwealth conference, where he denounces South Africa's apartheid government. South Africa withdraws from the Commonwealth.

1962
The Conservatives lose nearly half their seats, leaving them with a minority government.

1963
The Conservatives lose the federal election to Lester B. Pearson's Liberal party. John remains leader of the Conservative party.

1965
The Maple Leaf flag is adopted despite John's vigorous objections.

1966
John is publicly embarrassed by Dalton Camp and his supporters.

1967
John loses the Conservative leadership. He's replaced by Robert Stanfield.

1969
Astronauts walk on the moon for the first time.

1971
John's brother, Elmer, dies.

1976
Olive dies.

1979
John dies.

them. John did not know what to do—one day he wanted to have the missiles, the next day he didn't. This indecisiveness was the final straw for many in his party. One of his cabinet ministers even told him, "You might as well know that the people of Canada have lost confidence in you, the party has lost confidence in you, and the cabinet has lost confidence in you. It is time you went."

Too stubborn to quit

Although many people thought he was going to retire, John was too stubborn to quit. Another election was held on February 5, 1963, and the prime minister was convinced he could win again. He toured Canada, going to rallies, giving speeches, and finding that he still had a lot of support, especially in the rural areas of Western Canada.

When the election was over, the Liberals had won 129 seats, while the Conservatives had held on to only 95. John and Olive had to move out of **24 Sussex Drive**, for Lester B. Pearson was now the prime minister. John wanted to remain as leader of the Progressive Conservatives, but by now he had made many enemies within his own party. They were determined to do whatever it took to get him out. In November 1966, John went to a ballroom at the Château Laurier hotel in Ottawa to give a speech to members. What he did not know was that **Dalton Camp**, one of his biggest rivals, had made sure that all the seats in the hall were filled with people who didn't want John to be leader anymore. As TV cameras watched, John made a passionate speech that he hoped would rally the Conservatives. The people in the audience did not clap or cheer, but just remained silent, with some of them even sitting on their hands. Toward the end of the speech, someone in the crowd shouted at John, "Sit down and shut up!" The scene soon turned wild, as the crowd started to boo and jeer John, who felt deeply embarrassed and betrayed.

All washed up?

Despite this treachery, John still didn't quit. A Conservative leadership race was held the following year, and John decided to fight to hold his job, even though he had no chance of winning. In the end, Diefenbaker finished in fifth place, while **Robert Stanfield** won the race and became the new leader of the Tories (a nickname for the Conservative party). John and his wife slipped out of a back door and climbed into their limousine. "I guess I'm all washed up, Olive," John said quietly.

Before she could answer, the driver exclaimed, "You'll never be washed up, Chief," which made everyone happy again.

In 1975, a folk combo called Stringband recorded "Dief Will Be the Chief Again," a song that paid tribute to John. It went a little somethin' like this:

"Dief is the Chief,
Dief is the Chief,
Dief will be the Chief again.
Everybody's happy back in '57
And nobody's happy since then.
There was law in the land,
Order in the home,
Swimming in the river back then.
But I know in my heart
That Dief will be the Chief
And a dollar worth
a dollar again."

The strange and sad story of the Avro Arrow

Canadians don't have too many conspiracy theories—we are probably too level-headed to believe wild stories and rumours. But there has been one story going around for nearly 50 years that refuses to go away. It's the strange story of the Avro Arrow.

This story begins in the 1950s, at the height of the Cold War. The Soviet Union was seen as a threat, and many thought Canada might be a target for Soviet airplanes that would fly over the Arctic to bomb our cities. The Canadian government decided that the country needed a plane that was fast, powerful, and unbeatable in the skies.

The government chose the A. V. Roe Company to build several hundred planes for the country, and over the next few years the Avro Arrow was designed, built, and tested in Canada. Canadian engineers developed the most advanced fighter aircraft of its era. It could fly at supersonic speeds (faster than the speed of sound). Thousands of men and women were involved in the construction of the Arrow. For them and many other Canadians it was a symbol of our country's technological ability.

But the project had big problems too. By the late 1950s, it was already behind schedule, and was coming in way over budget. Hundreds of millions of dollars had been spent on it, and so far only a few prototypes had flown. John was told he would need to spend another $800 million before Canada could get their fighter planes, and this was money the government felt it needed for other military priorities. Another factor was that the Soviet Union was now building missiles that could fly around the world, so it looked like they would not be using bombers if it came to war. Canadian and US advisers to the government insisted that made the Arrow obsolete. They convinced the prime minister that Canada needed US-made missiles for its defence. With all this in mind, the prime minister decided to cancel the Avro Arrow project.

Crawford Gordon, the head of A. V. Roe, had known for months that the government would likely cancel the project. In spite of that, he acted like he was shocked by the decision and immediately laid off nearly 15,000 company employees. Many Canadians were upset with John because of this decision. Over the years, lots of books and movies about the Avro Arrow have blamed the airplane's demise on a personal rivalry between Diefenbaker and Gordon. Others have suggested that the United States pressured the government to cancel the project because they feared the Arrow would be a better fighter plane than their own aircraft. There is conflicting evidence regarding these theories, but many people are convinced that they are true.

Sadly, once the project ended, the few Avro Arrows that had been built were scrapped. Only a few pieces from the planes survive in museums, but many Canadians are still proud of the Arrow and the amazing technological achievement it represents. Several engineers from the Arrow project later went on to work in the US space program.

For more information about the Avro Arrow, visit our website at www.jackfruitpress.com.

43

John was almost 72 years old, but wasn't ready to quit politics. He remained the member of Parliament for Prince Albert, and he kept raising issues that were important to him and criticizing both the Liberals and his fellow Conservatives. John was still very bitter over how he was treated by some of those Tories who opposed him, and he was not the type to forgive and forget. A few people stood with him, but the most important was his wife Olive.

Hail to the "Chief"

John soldiered on—a permanent fixture on the backbenches now. In 1979, to the surprise of few, he became the longest-sitting member, having been elected 13 times.

On August 16, 1979, just a month before his 84th birthday, John was found dead alone in his study. He had probably woken up at 5:30 a.m., as usual, and had a **heart attack** soon after. A friend found him at his desk with parliamentary papers in his hands.

Ten thousand people filed past his coffin as it lay in state in Ottawa. His body was taken slowly home to Saskatoon on a special train. Thousands of people waited for hours along the rail tracks. They waved, saluted, and cried, saying goodbye to their Chief.

John repaid their loyalty by leaving 240 acres of homestead land, originally owned by his parents and his uncle Ed, to the University of Saskatchewan to be preserved so future children could view a homestead as it was in pioneer days.

The spirit of an indomitable man

John is buried beside Olive on the grounds of the University of Saskatchewan, in the shade of the trees overlooking the South Saskatchewan River. Their coffins were completely enclosed in wet cement. Not to protect them from grave robbers, but to fulfill John's last wish. You see, John was afraid of worms.

A year later, Canada Post memorialized him with a 17¢ stamp. In 1999, Saskatchewan artist Rob Muench painted a large mural of the stamp on the side of the Willkommen Centre, in Humboldt, Saskatchewan.

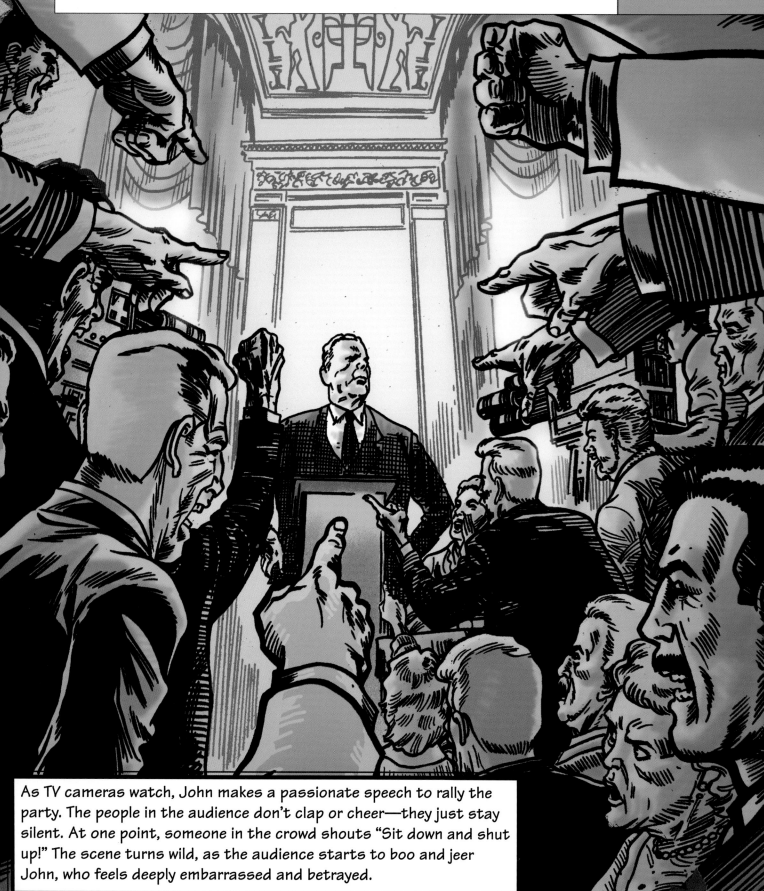

John's many enemies are determined to do whatever it takes to get rid of him. Showing up at a PC party convention, John is unaware that one of his rivals has filled the hall with people who don't want him to be leader anymore.

As TV cameras watch, John makes a passionate speech to rally the party. The people in the audience don't clap or cheer—they just stay silent. At one point, someone in the crowd shouts "Sit down and shut up!" The scene turns wild, as the audience starts to boo and jeer John, who feels deeply embarrassed and betrayed.

John Diefenbaker:

Most people who knew Canada's 13th prime minister remember him as the man who brought drama and excitement to the House of Commons. Some also remember him as a tireless advocate for farmers, aboriginal people, the underdog, and the disadvantaged.

John's main weapon in his battle on behalf of the underdog was his Bill of Rights. The document represents an important breakthrough because it asserts the equality of all Canadian citizens regardless of their social status, race, or country of origin. (As such, it foreshadowed the Canadian Charter of Rights and Freedoms, made into law just a few years later). If proclaiming the equality of all Canadians no longer seems necessary, it is because Canada has changed so much since that time. We have John Diefenbaker to thank for this.

John carried on his battle for equality and recognition in other important ways. He corrected a great national injustice by granting aboriginal people the right to vote in federal elections, and he appointed Canada's first First Nations senator. He also broke new ground by being the first PM to name women and citizens of "foreign" descent into his cabinet.

Dief's favourite motto, "One Canada," was far more than just an election slogan or rallying cry. It stood for a Canada that went far beyond being a home for its founding nations. It was about a Canada made up of diverse nationalities that converged here from all parts of the globe. A Canada that would become an example of multicultural peace and harmony for the world.

John Diefenbaker stands out in our history for two other important reasons. As Canada's leader at a time when the Cold War was in full

"One Canada for all Canadians."

He never stopped fighting

swing and most of the West was caught up in opposing the "Red menace," John refused to go along with the hysteria of the period and tried to preserve Canada's position as a peacemaker. He also stood out on the international scene because of his firm stance against **apartheid** in South Africa. Every bone in his body knew that denying human rights based on race was morally wrong and he spoke out against it.

Almost any Western Canadian will insist that John could have accomplished so much more had he been in power longer. His detractors will claim the opposite. They'll point out that the "Chief" did not live up to his promise. They'll complain that he took far too long to make important decisions, that many of his policies were muddled, and that he never really understood how to run a country. Because he never did manage to speak French, John didn't connect with French Canadians. For similar reasons, he also failed to endear himself to younger Canadians. His numerous solemn declarations of devotion to the British Empire now seem outdated and colonial. The same can be said of his rants against the Maple Leaf flag. He repeatedly warned us that our new flag was a desecration of our past and a negation of our future. Fortunately, Prime Minister Lester B. Pearson paid no attention to what John was saying. Pearson went on to give Canada a new identity that is now recognized and respected the world over.

But both John's fans and his opponents will readily admit that he never, ever forgot his vow to help the underdog. They will also agree that John Diefenbaker was a great actor, probably the greatest (and most entertaining) our political stage has seen so far. For that alone, we'll never forget him.

Timeline: The life and times of John Diefenbaker

YEAR	JOHN'S LIFE	EVENTS IN CANADA AND THE WORLD
1895	John is born in Neustadt, Ontario, on September 18.	
1896		Sir Charles Tupper becomes the sixth prime minister of Canada. Sir Wilfrid Laurier becomes the seventh prime minister.
1897	John's brother, Elmer, is born. His family moves to Ontario County, north of Whitby, Ont.	Wilfrid Laurier is knighted. Queen Victoria celebrates her diamond (60th) jubilee
1900	John's family moves to Todmorden, on the outskirts of Toronto, Ontario.	The head tax on Chinese immigrants is raised to $100 from the $50 set in 1885. The Commonwealth of Australia is formed.
1901		Queen Victoria dies.
1903	John and his family move close to Fort Carlton, Northwest Territories (now Saskatchewan).	Chinese head tax rises to $500—the equivalent of two years of labour—to discourage immigration from China.
1904	John tells his mom, "Someday I am going to be prime minister."	The Trans-Siberian Railway (1891–1904) is completed.
1905	John's family moves to Hague, Saskatchewan.	Alberta and Saskatchewan join Canada as provinces.
1906	John's family moves near Borden, Saskatchewan.	
1910	John's family moves to Saskatoon.	
1911		Sir Robert Laird Borden becomes the eighth prime minister.
1912	John begins studying at the University of Saskatchewan.	
1914		World War I (1914–1918) begins on August 1. Canada declares war on Germany in September.
1915	The student newspaper the *Sheaf* predicts that John will be Canada's leader of the Opposition in 40 years. John receives a BA from the University of Saskatchewan.	The first major battle is fought by Canadians during World War I. Known as the Battle of Ypres, in Belgium, it lasts from April 22 to May 25.
1916	John graduates with an MA in political science and economics, also from the University of Saskatchewan. He volunteers for service in World War I.	Manitoba amends its Election Act to allow women to vote in provincial elections.
1917	John is unable to continue serving in the war and is removed from service. He enrolls in law school at the University of Saskatchewan.	The conscription crisis occurs. Canadians fight in the battle of Vimy Ridge in France. A "temporary" income tax is introduced. The National Hockey League (NHL) is formed. The Russian Revolution ends with the Bolsheviks seizing power.
1918		White women are allowed to vote and eligible to be candidates in all provinces except Prince Edward Island and Quebec. World War I ends on Armistice Day, November 11. A worldwide influenza epidemic kills 25 million people.

48

More on the life and times of John Diefenbaker

YEAR	JOHN'S LIFE	EVENTS IN CANADA AND THE WORLD
1919	John is called to the Saskatchewan bar. He opens a law office in Wakaw.	The Winnipeg General Strike takes place from May 15 to June 26. The Treaty of Versailles is signed on June 28, officially ending World War I.
1920		Canada joins the League of Nations. Arthur Meighen becomes Canada's ninth prime minister. Women become eligible to sit in the House of Commons. The Progressive party forms.
1921	John meets Olive Freeman Palmer, his future second wife. He's elected alderman in Wakaw.	Agnes Macphail is the first woman elected to Parliament. William Lyon Mackenzie King becomes the 10th prime minister.
1922		White women are allowed to vote in Prince Edward Island. The Union of Soviet Socialist Republics (USSR) is formed from Russia and 14 other Soviet countries.
1924	John moves his law practice to Prince Albert, Saskatchewan.	The first national postal strike in Canada takes place.
1925	John is defeated in the federal election as a Conservative.	
1926	John is defeated in the second federal election in two years.	Arthur Meighen begins his second term as prime minister.
1929	John marries Edna Mae Brower. He is defeated in the provincial election.	The Judicial Committee of the Privy Council declares women to be legally "persons." The Wall Street stock market crashes, starting the 10-year-long Great Depression.
1930	John is named King's Counsel in the New Year's honours list.	Richard Bedford Bennett becomes the 11th prime minister. Cairine Wilson is the first female appointed senator.
1931		The Statute of Westminster gives Canada the power to change its own constitution, though it must still take place in the British Parliament.
1932		The Co-operative Commonwealth Federation (CCF) party is founded in Calgary.
1933	John is elected vice-president of the provincial Conservatives. He is defeated in the Prince Albert election for mayor.	Adolf Hitler is appointed chancellor of Germany.
1935	John is elected president of the provincial Conservative party.	The Bank of Canada is formed. Tommy Douglas wins a seat in the first election for the CCF party.
1936	He becomes leader of the Saskatchewan Conservatives.	The Canadian Broadcasting Corporation (CBC) is created. The Spanish Civil War begins (1936–1939). Germany hosts the Olympic Games in Berlin.
1937		King George VI is crowned in Great Britain.
1938	John fails to win a seat in the provincial election for the riding of Arm River.	Thousand Islands International Bridge at Ivy Lea, Ontario, opens. The German army marches into Austria and annexes it.
1939	John is named a candidate for the next federal election.	World War II begins on September 3 (1939–1945). Canada declares war on Germany on September 10.

49

Still more on the life and times of John Diefenbaker

YEAR	JOHN'S LIFE	EVENTS IN CANADA AND THE WORLD
1940	John wins his riding in Lake Centre in the federal election. He and Edna move to Ottawa.	The National Resources Mobilization Act is introduced. White women are given the right to vote in Quebec. Canada declares war on Italy on June 10.
1941		The unemployment insurance program begins. Canada, England, and the United States declare war on Japan.
1942	John runs for and loses the leadership of the federal Conservative party.	The Progressive and Conservative parties unite to become the Progressive Conservative (PC) party. Canada and the United States force citizens of Japanese descent to move inland, away from the West Coast.
1944		Allies land in Normandy, France, on D-Day, June 6.
1945	John's father dies. Edna is hospitalized. John wins a seat in the federal election.	The family allowance program ("baby bonus") begins. The United Nations is formed and Canada joins. Germany surrenders on May 8. The United States drops two atomic bombs on Japan. Japan surrenders on September 2.
1946	Edna is released from hospital.	
1948	John runs for leadership of the federal Progressive Conservative (PC) party and loses.	Louis St. Laurent becomes the 12th prime minister. South Africa introduces apartheid. A war (1948–1949) between Israeli and Arab forces from Egypt, Syria, Transjordan (later Jordan), Lebanon, and Iraq begins.
1949	John wins his seat in the federal election.	Newfoundland becomes a province. The North Atlantic Treaty Organization is created; Canada joins.
1950	John learns that Edna is suffering from acute lymphatic leukemia.	The Korean War begins (1950–53): North Korea invades South Korea.
1951	Edna dies in Saskatoon.	
1952	John wins his riding in the federal election.	King George VI dies and is succeeded by his daughter, who becomes Queen Elizabeth II
1953	John wins in the federal election. He marries widow Olive Freeman Palmer.	Fidel Castro begins a revolution in Cuba.
1956	John is elected leader of the PC party.	The Suez War takes place: Great Britain and France attack Egypt to maintain international control of the Suez Canal.
1957	John becomes the 13th prime minister. He attends the Commonwealth Prime Ministers' Conference in London. John addresses the UN.	Ellen Fairclough becomes Canada's first female cabinet minister. Lester Pearson wins the Nobel Peace Prize. The USSR launches the first two earth satellites: Sputnik I and II. The Vietnam War begins (1957-1975): North Vietnam forces attack South Vietnam and win control of it.
1958	John is re-elected as PM. John and Olive tour Commonwealth countries.	James Gladstone is appointed Canada's first First Nations senator. CBC begins TV broadcasts from coast to coast. Canada's Bill of Rights is introduced.
1959	John cancels the development of the Avro Arrow CF-105. He appoints Georges Vanier as the first French-Canadian governor general.	Construction of the South Saskatchewan Dam starts. Queen Elizabeth II tours Canada. Fidel Castro becomes premier and dictator of Cuba.

Even more on the life and times of John Diefenbaker

YEAR	JOHN'S LIFE	EVENTS IN CANADA AND THE WORLD
1960	John addresses the UN on disarmament.	First Nations peoples are granted the right to vote. The Canadian Bill of Rights is passed.
1961	John leads the Commonwealth Prime Ministers' Conference. He establishes the Royal Commission on Health Services. His mother, Mary, dies.	The CCF party changes its name to the New Democratic Party. Cuban exiles unsuccessfully invade Cuba at the Bay of Pigs. South Africa withdraws from the Commonwealth. The Berlin Wall is built.
1962	John wins the election but his party is reduced to a minority government.	The Canadian dollar drops to 92.5¢ US. The last execution in Canada takes place. US president Kennedy orders a naval quarantine of Cuba, bringing the world to the brink of nuclear war.
1963	John ends his term as prime minister and becomes leader of the Opposition.	Lester B. Pearson becomes the 14th prime minister. The Royal Commission on Bilingualism and Biculturalism begins. US president Kennedy is assassinated in Dallas, Texas.
1964		Nelson Mandela is jailed for opposing apartheid in South Africa.
1965	John wins his seat in the federal election, the 25th anniversary of his election to Parliament.	The new Maple Leaf flag is adopted. The Canada Pension Plan is established.
1966	John refuses to resign as leader of the PC party.	Universal medical care is granted. The CBC begins colour television broadcasts. Indira Gandhi becomes prime minister of India.
1967	John loses the leadership of the PC party to Robert Stanfield. He serves his last day as leader of the Opposition on July 7.	Canada celebrates the 100th anniversary of Confederation. French president De Gaulle visits Montreal and exclaims *Vive le Québec libre!* ("Long live free Quebec!"). The Six Day War takes place between Israel and Egypt, Jordan, and Syria.
1968		Lincoln MacCauley Alexander becomes the first black MP. Pierre Elliott Trudeau becomes the 15th prime minister. René Lévesque founds the separatist Parti Québécois. US civil rights leader Martin Luther King is assassinated.
1969		US astronaut Neil Armstrong walks on the moon.
1970		Front de libération du Québec (FLQ) terrorists kidnap two officials.
1971	John's brother, Elmer, dies.	
1972	John wins his seat in the federal election after campaigning by helicopter.	Muriel McQueen Fergusson is appointed the first female speaker of the Senate.
1974	John becomes the first MP to be sworn in 12 times.	US president Nixon resigns due to the Watergate scandal: he tried to conceal a break-in of the rival Democratic party's headquarters.
1976	John's second wife, Olive, dies on December 22 in Ottawa.	The summer Olympics are held in Montreal. René Lévesque, leader of the Parti Québécois, becomes premier of Quebec.
1979	John is elected MP for the 13th time. He dies on August 16 in his Ottawa home at the age of 83.	Joe Clark becomes the 16th prime minister. Margaret Thatcher becomes the first female prime minister of Great Britain.

Glossary: words and facts you might want to know

Korean War (1950–1953): the war that began when North Korea attacked South Korea. Canada, as part of the United Nations force, fought on South Korea's side. The war expanded when China and the USSR entered the conflict to help North Korea. The war ended as a stalemate; neither side won or lost. Negotiations led to a cease-fire in 1951 and a formal agreement to end the fighting in 1953. No peace treaty has yet been signed.

Laurier, Sir Wilfrid (1841–1911): Canada's seventh prime minister (1896–1911) and the first one who was a French Canadian.

leukemia: a broad term covering a group of diseases. It is a cancer that starts in blood-forming tissue such as bone marrow and causes large numbers of white blood cells to be produced and overflow into the circulating blood stream.

Liberal party: political party that adopted its name after Confederation in 1867. It was formed from the union of the pre-Confederation Reform party (of what is now Ontario) and the Parti rouge (in present-day Quebec).

Macdonald, Sir John A. (1815–1891): Canada's first prime minister (1867–1873, 1878–1891). Born in Scotland, he moved to Upper Canada with his family in 1820. He trained and worked as a lawyer before becoming involved in politics. He spent many years working on bringing the Province of Canada and the Maritime provinces together. On July 1, 1867, his dream came true with the creation of the Dominion of Canada. He died while in office in Ottawa.

Mandela, Nelson (1918–): jailed for resisting South Africa's program of apartheid from 1962 to 1990. During his years in prison, he became a symbol of resistance as the anti-apartheid movement gathered strength. After his release, he continued his life's work to see apartheid end, which happened in 1993.

manslaughter: a crime committed "in the heat of passion"; meaning that the person who caused the death was so stirred up that the law accepts this as the reason. Manslaughter is also when someone acts irresponsibly and causes death.

member of Parliament (MP): politician who is elected to sit in the House of Commons. During a general election, the country is divided up into ridings. Voters in each riding elect one candidate to represent them in the government as their MP.

Métis: a person whose ancestry is half First Nations and half French Canadian. Métis culture combines both backgrounds.

mock parliament: activity in which non-politicians—usually students—act as if they are conducting business in the House of Commons. This provides an opportunity to learn about the workings of the Canadian government.

Northwest Mounted Police (NWMP): formed in 1873 by the government of Canada to keep law and order in the Northwest Territories. In 1919, the name of the force was changed to the Royal Canadian Mounted Police (RCMP), which still exists today as Canada's federal police force.

Northwest Rebellion (1885): the second rebellion led by Louis Riel. By the 1880s, European and other settlers were moving into the area now known as Saskatchewan, and the Métis saw their traditional lifestyle threatened. First Nations people had signed treaties giving up claim to all of the territory and agreeing to live on reserves. When the Canadian government did not live up to its end of the deal, the Métis of Saskatchewan asked Louis Riel to help them. He set up a provisional government that was eventually overthrown by Canadian soldiers. Riel surrendered and was hanged for treason.

nuclear warheads: weapons that get their destructive force from the reactions of nuclear fission or fusion. They're much more powerful than conventional explosives, and a single weapon is capable of destroying an entire city.

Opposition leader: in Canada's parliamentary system, the leader of the largest party not in government. The leader of the Opposition manages a rival government known as the shadow cabinet.

Palmer, Carolyn (1934–): stepdaughter of John Diefenbaker. When she was 18, her mother, Olive Freeman Palmer, married John.

Palmer, Olive Freeman (1902–1976): John Diefenbaker's second wife. They married in 1953, three years before John won the PC party leadership. John had been widowed when his first wife, Edna Mae Brower, died.

More words and facts you might want to know

Pearson, Lester B. (1897–1972): Canada's 14th prime minister (1963–1968). He was a man of several careers before he entered politics, including history professor, secretary in the Canadian High Commission in London during World War II, ambassador to the United States, and deputy minister of external affairs. He received the Nobel Peace Prize in 1957.

Progressive Conservative (PC) party: name of the Conservative Party of Canada following its union with some members of the farm-focused Progressive party in 1942. In 2004, the party merged with the Canadian Alliance to become the new Conservative party.

riding: or constituency. It is the geographical area that is represented by an MP in the House of Commons. Provinces and territories are also divided up into ridings so that a representative is elected to represent the people as a member of the provincial or territory legislative assemblies.

riding the rods: getting free transportation by riding railroad cars. Specifically, "riding the rods" meant riding underneath the car on its structural rods. Riding the rods or riding the deck (riding on top of a car) was very dangerous; riding inside a car was preferred. Eventually, railroads began using cars without structural rods underneath.

St. Laurent, Louis (1882–1973): Canada's 12th prime minister (1948—1957). In 1941, while working as a lawyer in Quebec, he was invited by William Lyon Mackenzie King to become minister of justice. He became King's successor as leader of the Liberal party. He sent Canadian troops to fight for the United Nations in Korea.

seat in Parliament: place where an MP sits in the House of Commons, part of Canada's Parliament. Parliament is the national legislature in Canada. It has two houses: an upper house called the Senate and a lower house called the House of Commons. Senators are appointed by the governor general but the Canadian people elect their representatives to the House of Commons.

Stanfield, Robert (1914–2003): leader of the federal PC party (1967–1976) and successor to John Diefenbaker. Born in Truro, Nova Scotia, he became the province's premier in 1956, serving four terms before becoming involved in federal politics. He suffered three electoral defeats against Pierre Trudeau's Liberals before retiring.

Stornoway: official residence of the federal leader of the Opposition. Located at 541 Acadia Avenue in Rockcliffe Park, near Ottawa, it has been owned by the federal government since 1970.

tuberculosis: often fatal disease of the lungs, skeletal system, kidneys, and lymph nodes. It was once the disease of poor people who lived in crowded, unsanitary conditions. Its death toll decreased when steps were taken to clean up the cities in the late 1800s. Infected people recovered from the disease in special hospitals called sanatoria.

24 Sussex Drive: in Ottawa, the official residence of the prime minister of Canada since 1951. The first prime minister to live there was Louis St. Laurent. The house was built in 1866.

unemployment: a situation in which people who want and are able to work cannot find a job.

United Nations (UN): an organization that works for international peace and security. The UN provides a place for representatives of countries to meet and settle their problems peacefully. It was established in 1945 at the end of World War II.

visitors' gallery: also known as the public gallery of the Senate and the House of Commons. When the Senate or the House of Commons are sitting, visitors may watch the proceedings from the galleries.

weapons of mass destruction (WMD): weapons capable of destroying large areas and/or killing many people. They include nuclear, biological, chemical, and radiological weapons.

World War I (1914–1918): also known as the First World War or the Great War. It was a conflict that involved most of Europe as well as Russia, the United States, the Middle East, and other regions. The war pitted the Central Powers (mainly Germany, Austria-Hungary, and Turkey) against the Allies (mainly France, Great Britain (including Canada), Russia, Italy, Japan and, from 1917, the United States). It ended with the defeat of the Central Powers.

For more information on the terms listed in this glossary, visit www.jackfruitpress.com

Index

A

aboriginal people. *See* First Nations peoples
Acadians, 38, 52
apartheid, 41, 47, 50, 51, 52, 54
Atherton, Alfred John. *See* Canoe River case
Avro Arrow, 40, 41, 43, 52

B

Bennett, R. B., 26, 49
Bill of Rights, 23, 35, 38, 46, 50, 51, 52
Blood Reserve, 38, 52
Bomarc missiles, 41, 42, 52
Brower, Edna Mae, 25, 26, 29, 30, 32, 49, 50, 52, 54
budget deficit, 38, 52

C

cabinet, 6, 36, 42, 46, 52, 53
Camp, Dalton, 41, 42, 52
Campbell, Maria, 22, 52
Canadian dollar, value of, 38, 42, 51
Canoe River case, 29, 30, 31, 32, 33
Charter of Rights and Freedoms, 46, 52
Château Laurier, 42
civil liberties, 23, 38, 46, 52
civil servant, 9, 32, 52
Cold War, 37, 43, 46, 52
communist, 37, 52
Confederation, 12, 51
conscription, 9, 29, 48, 53
Conservative party. *See* Progressive Conservative party
Co-operative Commonwealth Federation (CCF) party, 27, 36, 49, 51
criminal negligence, 22, 53
Crown Assets Disposal Corporation, 36, 53
Crown prosecutor, 31, 32, 53
Cuban missile crisis, 37, 51

D

Davis, T. C., 26
death penalty, 22, 51
democracy, 53
Diefenbaker, Elmer, 8, 9, 10, 12, 18, 22, 32, 33, 41, 48, 51
Diefenbaker, John George
    and equal rights, 6, 23, 29, 38, 46, 47
    birth, 9, 10, 48
    death, 6, 41, 44, 51
    "Dief the Chief", 6, 35, 42, 44, 47
    enemies, 6, 22, 25, 26, 33, 38, 42, 45, 47
    German heritage, 6, 9, 10, 25, 38
    law practice, 5, 20, 21, 22, 23, 25, 26, 32, 49
    marriages, 25, 33
    military service, 18
    quotations, 6, 14, 15, 16, 22, 23, 25, 31, 35, 39, 46
    ridings, 25, 26, 32, 33, 49, 50
    school, 15, 16, 18, 48
    speaking style, 5, 6, 7, 28, 29, 46
Diefenbaker, Mary Bannerman, 5, 9, 10, 11, 12, 16, 18, 29, 35, 41, 48, 51
Diefenbaker, William Thomas, 8, 9, 10, 11, 12, 15, 18, 29, 50
Diefenbucks, 35, 38
Dirty '30s, 27
Douglas, Tommy, 27, 49
Drew, George, 33, 53
Dumont, Gabriel, 12, 53

E

economic depression, 25, 26, 27, 49, 53
election of 1958, 6, 36, 38, 50

F

Fairclough, Ellen Louks, 35, 36, 50, 53
First Nations peoples, 6, 11, 12, 22, 29, 35, 38, 46, 50, 51, 52, 53, 54

G

gerrymandering, 32, 33, 53
Gladstone, James, 35, 38, 50, 53
Gordon, Crawford, 40, 43
governor general, 50, 55
Great Depression, the. *See* economic depression

H

heart attack, 44, 53
homestead, 12, 44
House of Commons, 7, 15, 28, 29, 46, 49, 52, 53, 54, 55

J

Japanese Canadians, 6, 23, 29, 50
Jehovah's Witnesses, 23, 29, 53

K

Kennedy, John F., 37, 51, 53
King, William Lyon Mackenzie, 6, 9, 49, 53, 55
Korean War, 29, 30, 31, 32, 50, 54, 55

L

Laurier, Sir Wilfrid, 9, 14, 15, 16, 48, 54
leukemia, 29, 30, 50, 52, 54
Liberal party, 9, 21, 22, 32, 35, 36, 38, 41, 42, 44, 54, 55

M

Macdonald, Sir John A., 15, 54
majority government, 6, 35, 36
Mandela, Nelson, 23, 51, 54
manslaughter, 31, 54
McLorg, E. A. C., 21
member of Parliament, 23, 29, 36, 44, 51, 53, 54, 55
Métis, 12, 22, 52, 54
minority government, 41, 51
mock parliament, 16, 54
Muench, Rob, 44

N

Neustadt, Ontario, 9, 10, 48
Northwest Mounted Police, 11, 12, 54
Northwest Rebellion, 12, 53, 54
Northwest Territories, 8, 10, 48, 53, 54.
    See also Saskatchewan
nuclear warheads, 37, 41, 52, 54

O

On-to-Ottawa Trek, 25, 26
105th Saskatoon Fusiliers, 15, 18
One Canada, 29, 46
Opposition leader, 15, 16, 24, 29, 32, 35, 41, 42, 45, 48, 50, 51, 54, 55
Ottawa, Ontario, 15, 23, 25, 26, 27, 29, 32, 38, 40, 42, 44, 50, 51, 54, 55

P

Palmer, Carolyn, 32, 54
Palmer, Olive Freeman, 29, 32, 36, 41, 42, 44, 49, 50, 51, 54
Parliament Hill, 25, 26, 27, 34, 36
Pearson, Lester B., 38, 42, 47, 50, 51, 55
Prairies, the, 12, 13, 27, 52
Progressive Conservative party, 9, 24, 25, 26, 29, 33, 35, 36, 38, 41, 42, 44, 49, 50, 52, 53, 55

R

riding the rods, 26, 27, 55
ridings, 32, 53, 54, 55
Rupert's Land, 12

S

Sable Island ponies, 35, 36, 38
St. Laurent, Louis, 35, 50, 55
Saskatchewan
    Fort Carlton, 10, 12, 48
    Lake Centre, 26, 32, 50
    Prince Albert, 25, 26, 32, 33, 44, 49
    Saskatoon, 15, 16, 18, 21, 25, 32, 35, 44, 48, 50
    Wakaw, 21, 25, 49
seat in Parliament, 5, 55
Senate, 35, 38, 52, 55
Sheaf, the, 15, 16, 48
Social Credit party, 27, 32, 36
Stanfield, Robert, 41, 42, 51, 55
Stornoway, 35, 55

T

Tiefengrund schoolhouse, 10
Toronto, Ontario, 10, 32, 48
Trudeau, Pierre Elliott, 51, 55
tuberculosis, 9, 10, 55
24 Sussex Drive, 42, 55

U

unemployment, 27, 38, 50, 55
United Nations (UN), 29, 30, 50, 54, 55
University of Saskatchewan, 15, 16, 18, 44, 48, 52

V

visitors' gallery, 15, 29, 55

W

weapons of mass destruction, 37, 41, 52, 54, 55
work camps, 25, 26, 27
World War I, 15, 18, 19, 25, 48, 49, 53, 55
World War II, 25, 27, 29, 49, 52, 53, 55